War Bride of Wem

*The Life
of
Margaret Downes Hickenbottom*

by
Sandy Benson Castillo

Azalea Art Press
Sonoma . California

All rights reserved.
© 2024 by Sandy Benson Castillo

ISBN: 978-1-943471-81-2

This work is a truthful recollection of actual events in Margaret Downes Hickenbottom's life. It reflects my present recollections of her experiences over time, although some events have been compressed, and some dialogue has been recreated.

For Keith, Barry, Gerri,
and the rest of Margaret's family

> Two roads diverged in a wood
> and I—I took the one less traveled by,
> and that has made all the difference.
>
> *—Robert Frost, "Roads"*

Margaret Thorley Hickenbottom set sail from England at age 19—a young war bride—to join her husband in America. She, too, "ventured off the beaten path... to blaze a new trail..."

Contents

Introduction	*i*
Part One **E. M. H.**	**1**
Family Photographs	*13*
Paintings by *Margaret Downes Hickenbottom*	*23*
Memorabilia	*33*
Part Two **Wem, England**	**39**
Epilogue	*51*
We Were English War Brides	*55*
Resources / References	*53*
Dates of Importance	*56*
Acknowledgments	*61*
Other Books of Interest	*63*
About the Author	*65*
Contact	*66*

Evelyn Margaret Thorley Downes Hickenbottom
(by Emi Koch, 1945, Wem, England)

Introduction

War Bride of Wem: The Life of Margaret Downes Hickenbottom is a memoir I have written about Margaret Hickenbottom, the mother of my friend, Keith Hickenbottom.

Her story came to mind on a Saturday after a full day of helping Keith empty his mother's possessions from her home. We removed both household goods and personal items from her kitchen cabinets, wardrobe dressers, dining room hutch, art room, the back porch storage shed packed full with her painted artworks on canvas, and where her backyard gnomes, bird feeders and garden tools lay.

Margaret's home was being made ready to sell. I recall thinking and feeling, *I am an observer of her life, on the outside looking in*, and I began wondering about Margaret's life in England, and later, in America as I touched the objects that had been so dear to her. It stayed on my mind. It was as if her life was passing in front of me showing me where she was from and what she did during her life. I recall thinking that in her long life Margaret had been industrious, was an accomplished artist, and was a very energetic person in all her years on earth.

On September 21, 2022, I began writing down my thoughts and feelings to somehow make sense of the urgency I felt to write about Margaret. Before long, I had typed six pages of my observations about her life and the thoughts in my imagination.

Margaret was 95 years of age when we first met on September 5, 2021—the occasion of her birthday. In Chapter One, I give a picture of Margaret from my memories gleaned from knowing her for one year.

Looking back, I recall a previous conversation held with Margaret when she said to me that she once lived in Wem, England. Being curious, I searched Wem on the internet and, based on that research, began developing a story about her life.

In Chapter Two I write about Wem from resources that are indicated in the References at the back of this book. It is hoped Margaret's family will find my story an interesting read, and find facts not known before.

I include reproductions of some of Margaret's known fine art original works, her treasured collections, and other items that caught my attention when at Margaret's home. This was on more than one occasion while helping Keith to box up items left behind on her passing, October 12, 2022.

Margaret made a good impression on me. She was sweet and kind-hearted and mindfully sharp. In later months after our first meeting, I saw that illness and age were catching up on her. Her demise was sad for all of us — for her family and for me — to see. I recall seeing the twinkle in her brown eyes and sweet smile on her face, still fair in her later years of life. As we talked during my visits with her at her son Keith's home, she spoke of feeling cold — of her aches and pains as people will — and she spoke of her wish to return to Wem, England.

War Bride of Wem: The Life of Margaret Downes Hickenbottom is my observation and my point of view of Margaret. It is not a book on every aspect of Margaret's life be it as a young girl living in Wem, or as a young wife with Forrest, her husband of 61 years, or during the time she was a mother to her young sons Keith, Barry, and Jeffrey when they were young boys. Rather, it speaks of a time when Margaret had grown old at 95 years of age.

My observations of her stem from my visits with her, our conversations, and a little of my imagination as to how it may have been for her in her lifetime.

I have mentioned that Margaret was industrious—she was! She repaired many broken objects, such as the reproductions shown here in print. I sense she must have painstakingly glued-back the broken parts of a Wem souvenir dish.

She was artistic—she was! Apart from the known examples of original fine art her friends and family may have in their possession, her known artworks are shown. She loved beautiful ceramics and other collectibles as evidenced by her treasured collections—a variety of paired candlesticks, tall and short flower ceramic vases, artistically-designed matching teacups and saucers, and a formal dinnerware set for twelve each stamped: *Made In England*.

Energetic—she was! Margaret loved to sew clothing for herself and for children as evidenced by a box packed full of McCall and Simplicity patterns. These were boxed up on the floor next to an extensive magazine and hardbound book collection denoting a wide range of interests throughout her lifetime.

Margaret, at 96, has now left her life, her loved ones, and her possessions. She is free and unencumbered. I like thinking I have honored her in my memoir and her importance as a human being on the eve of her demise. We all can remember her now in Spirit.

—**Sandy Benson Castillo**
April 2024

*All truths are easy to understand
once they are discovered;
the point is to discover them.*

—Galileo Galilei

War Bride of Wem

The Life of Margaret Downes Hickenbottom

Young Brides

They have chosen their partners, they're proud and they're glad of their Aussie, their Yank, or Canadian lad.

From parents and friends and their land they'll depart. What a great step for a very young heart.

Off to a country unknown and untried to learn other methods and customs beside.

Even their partners at first must be shared with his people and friends who have waited and cared.

These young brides must take courage and continue along. For they can't run back home when small matters go wrong.

They will speak for this land by behavior and deed. Must earn their acceptance and honor their breed.

Good luck and God Bless them these pioneer brides. And give them fine children the best of both sides.

Text from a clipping from an English newspaper, author unknown, circa 1945.

PART ONE
E.M.H.

**Life is what happens
when you are busy making other plans.**

—John Lennon

On this, her recent birthday, in the year 2022, Evelyn Margaret Thorley Downes Hickenbottom is 96 years of age. Though frail and laden with telling signs of confusion due to aging and memory loss, we engage in conversation during my visits with her while she lives, temporarily, at her son Keith's home.

She speaks to me of fond memories when, as a young girl, she enjoyed her family, her home, and of wishing to return to her beloved birthplace, Wem, County District of Shropshire, England — a home shared with nine older siblings and her parents.

But Wem is far away and there are few remaining families who could welcome her back, as her siblings are gone having passed away from life years ago. Yet, recently, I've learned that her nephews, Edward Blake (son of Margaret's sister, Ethel) and George Downes (son of Arthur Downes, Margaret's brother) are living in England. Margaret's life, a life she later shared upon her marriage to Forrest Richard Hickenbottom, continues.

Margaret, the name she went by, met Forrest Hickenbottom in 1944 in Wem while Forrest was stationed there prior to the June 6, 1944, WWII invasion of Normandy in France. Forrest was assigned to the United States Army's 457th Engineer Depot Company as a big equipment crane operator while in the European Theatre of Operations.

It is believed Forrest and Margaret met in Wem when Margaret worked for the Axillary Fire Service within the National Fire Service as well as in nearby Stoke-On-Trent, England. The fire station was then located at the rear of the Town Hall where social activities were held.

Born on September 5, 1926, in Wem, England, County District of Shropshire, Margaret was then 18 years of age. Forrest, born October 12, 1921, in Union Town, Ohio, was 24. Margaret's brown eyes, mahogany brown hair, fair complexion, and five-foot two-inch height caught his attention. She took notice of Forrest for his handsome good looks and his good-hearted nature.

A new life is on the horizon for Margaret when she and Forrest meet and marry a year later on September 22, 1945, in Stoke-On-Trent. After the war is over, Forrest returns to the United States in January, 1946. Now a "War Bride," Margaret leaves Wem the following April after the May 9, 1945, surrender of Germany to the Allies in Berlin, sailing on the William H. Holbrook—known as a 'Kaiser cork'—out of Southampton, England for America.

On her Atlantic Ocean voyage, Margaret sees the Queen Mary as it steams back toward England for its next load of war brides. After nine days at sea and seasick for seven, Margaret arrives at the harbor of New York City, wherein Forrest greets his young bride.

They soon leave for Union Town, Ohio, where they will live until she is 36 years of age. During this time, she becomes a homemaker, mother, and farm rancher. Margaret finds that the art of canning and freezing a wide variety of fruits and vegetables grown by Forrest on their Ohio farm ranch is rewarding work.

A perpetually proper English lady, Margaret was the 10th and last child born to her parents Alfred Downes (1878—1933) and Eleanor Mary Thorley (1882—1969), both of England. Alfred's mother birth name was Emma. Born in 1853, she died in 1903. We do not know Emma's last name. She is known only as Emma Downes — "a single servant woman of Horton." *(Ref. 1)*. Margaret's siblings were, in order of birth, Charles, Harry, Percy, Mona, Walter, Ethel, Arthur, Nellie, and Edna.

In a long-kept clipped newspaper photo found among Margaret's filed documents, it is reported that at her wedding she wore a turquoise blue "frock" with navy blue accessories, carrying in her hands a white prayer book. While the turquoise blue dress is long gone, the white prayer book remains with Margaret.

Upon her marriage to Forrest, Margaret becomes the daughter-in-law of William Burdette Hickenbottom and Clara Tennessee Stiubs of Ohio. Forrest is one of five children and the firstborn son of three boys.

During Margaret's life as a wife, homemaker, and mother, she is also a fine arts painter. Courses in art are taken while she and Forrest live in Simi Valley, California, during 1969 and 1970. Margaret preserves her memories of England in scenes of 'Home' onto the canvas, including scenes of quaint English cottages and barns, landscapes, blue skies, neighbors in the street, and sheep on the hillsides.

She enjoys and revels at painting, using her oils and watercolor paints in a myriad of colors. When completed, each is framed with quality wood, each caressing a work of art. It's been thought by some that Margaret's artistic talent is inherited from her Thorley family side; however, we know she receives formal training while living in Simi Valley.

Margaret attends various art classes in later years as evidenced by the *Certificates Of Completion in Art* awarded while in Simi Valley. Six certificates were awarded to Margaret dated from January 27, 1966 to June 4, 1968, for "Advanced Drawing and Painting" in Simi Valley Unified School District for both evening and day classes. She will often sign her art, sometimes using only her initials, E.M.H., as she hones her skill in fine arts.

Her first award is an Honorable Mention at the Tierra Adorada District 14 Fine Arts Festival of which the date is unknown. A favorite artwork of hers wins 4th Place and is awarded on April 26, 2012. At age 56, on March 25, 1982, Margaret earns her first award for a painting in the watercolor category.

Margaret's painting days end later in her life when at about age 90 she lays down her artist's paint brush for the last time. Her art pens and brushes are stored away, as her arthritic hands and sore joints will not allow for yet another stroke upon the canvas.

She has become prone to falls due to a decline in health and is dependent on others to help her in daily living. A recent fall takes her from her home in Cameron Park, California to the nearby hospital's emergency room. Today she is recovering in a skilled nursing care facility and may not return to her home on Garden Lane in

Cameron Park, her beloved home shared with Forrest until his passing in 2006 at age 84.

Forrest and Margaret begin their lives together in their comfortable ranch home in Union Town, Ohio, where Forrest was born and raised. Born on October 13, 1921, Forrest is a Levi-wearing strip coal miner and crane mechanic on a dragline in the open pit coal mine in Union Town. He is also a home farmer/rancher prior to his draft into the Army at the start of WWII.

His father, William Burdette Hickenbottom and his mother, Clara Tennessee Stiubs—both from Eastern Ohio and of English backgrounds—are farmer/ranchers. Forrest decides early on he does not want his three sons, Keith and Barry and Jeffrey, to follow him by working in the coal mines of Ohio, and in 1962, Forrest moves Margaret and their three young sons to Simi Valley, California. The Aerospace Program in America is underway and jobs are available to people who would apply from all parts of the United States.

In Simi Valley, Forrest secures work at Rocketdyne in the Engineering Department for

Inspections at the Lunar Excursion Module known as LEM. With the downsizing of the Aerospace program in the 1970s, he secures work at the Rancho Simi Park and Recreation Department as Park Groundskeeper. He also starts a pool cleaning business and becomes a realtor in a Century 21 office.

Margaret and Forrest have three children — all boys — Keith, Barry, and Jeffrey. All three enjoy their younger years in Ohio playing rough-and-tumble games, roughhousing with each other, and forming close bonds as brothers. Family life is good for the Hickenbottoms.

After the first generation Hickenbottom children are gone from home, Margaret begins dreaming of returning to her beloved birthplace — Wem, England. She stays in touch by telephoning long-distance regularly with her nephew, Edward Blake, son of her sister, Ethel. Born in 1957, Edward resides in Wem and maintains weekly contact with Margaret.

In 1987, when sons Keith, Barry, and Jeffrey have grown up and moved away from home, Forrest retires. He and Margaret then move to

Clearlake, California. In 1998, Forrest and Margaret move yet again, this time to a quaint and quiet corner house in the newly-established County Club Estates on Garden Circle across the street from Cameron Park Country Club—their last home together. After their 61 years of marriage, Forrest dies in 2006.

Lately, Margaret cries out to Keith, saying she wants to return to Wem. "Take me to the train station," she pleads to Keith the other day before her recent fall, adding, "I want to go to Wem."

Keith tells her she cannot go, saying with a twinkle in his blue eyes, and a half cautionary smile, "Mom, the trains aren't running today."

Margaret, diagnosed with dementia and Alzheimer's disease, has a dreaded malady of the aged. At age 96, she struggles daily in a fight to stay in control of her independence. In a recent fall, Margaret is taken to the nearby hospital's Emergency Room. Subsequent health evaluation deems it necessary for Margaret to be placed in a skilled nursing care facility. After a complete two-week medical evaluation and health care received at the facility, Margaret transfers into a permanent care facility located in a neighborhood setting near Keith's home.

Keith, older brother to Barry and Jeffrey, is married to his wife Chris for 33 years before their union ends in divorce. Now a bachelor, Keith works as a General Building Contractor for an agricultural firm in Sacramento, California. Barry, currently retired from a military defense department of the U.S. government, lives with his wife, Gerri, in Southern California. Jeffrey's occupation was in the computer industry. The youngest of the three Hickenbottom boys, Jeffrey, previously married to Kathryn, succumbed to a heart attack at age 60 in 2014. Both Keith and Barry, with Gerri, Chris, and Kathryn's help, share in overseeing the details of caring for Margaret's health care in these her later years of life.

Second generation Hickenbottoms — the first grandchildren to Margaret and Forrest — are Brett Forrest and Kelsey Blair, both children of Keith and Chris's. Barry's two sons are Joel and Jon. Jeffrey's two daughters are Sara and Jessica.

The third generation Hickenbottoms are Margaret's and Forrest's great-grandchildren, Addie and Calvin, daughter and son of Kelsey's. James and Cayden, sons of Sara, all play a role in joy for Margaret to love and behold.

Not met with joy but with sadness, Keith, Barry, and Gerri must now pack up Margaret's possessions while gathering personal belongings and objects of comfort for Margaret in anticipation of her move to the permanent care facility.

Margaret's treasured possessions—the special drinking glasses and coffee mugs used at family gatherings; the fine English China Margaret loved so much; her English designer serving bowls; her flower-etched candlestick holders; her *Made In England* floral teacups each with matching saucer; her dozen or so birdfeeders in her garden and hanging from the outside eaves; the assortment of FTD now-empty flower vases dating back to happy years; a wide variety of teapots also *Made In England* resting on the inside kitchen sill; and the fine Ethan Allen furniture all the family enjoyed—all say her life was a contented one.

Margaret has lived a good life. She made a home for her husband and family. She shared her life and love for her husband and children, staying by his side all his life, and by raising her children in the only way she knew. She could have been strict and stern, and opinionated, and outspoken. And she was known—her presence, herself alone.

Wem, a magical place, exists. It is 5,250 miles from where Margaret is today. But, to hear Margaret speak of it, it is not extremely far. She wants to go there now. One day she will in her sweet, ladylike Spirit—when it is her time to leave her life on earth, when she moves to the other side, passing on into Eternal Rest.

Family Photographs

E. Downes & Sons
Eleanor M. Downes, owner
(Newsagent, Tobacconist, Confectioner)
27 Aston Street
Wem, England

This detail from the portrait
of Margaret Downes Hickenbottom in the front
of this book shows the signature of Emi Koch.

Emi Koch was a German P.O.W. while in Wem
in 1945. It is not known how it came about
that the artist could have liberties, unless the
English government had a program of activities
while he was in captivity.

No one seems to know the full history.

Margaret & Forrest Hickenbottom
Wedding Photo

Forrest & Margaret Hickenbottom
Wedding Photo

Margaret making sweet rolls
adding a topping of candies

Margaret beside her waterscape
at her Cameron Park home

**Margaret in rollers
painting the Hickenbottom mailbox**

The Hickenbottom Boys
(L-R) Jeffrey, Keith, & Barry

**(L-R)
Chris, Keith, Kathryn, Jeffrey, Gerri, Barry,
Margaret & Forest
in front center row**

Paintings
by
Margaret Downes Hickenbottom

**English Farm
1989**

**Hick's Place
1987**

Blue Dreams
1967

Forrest Gate
2002

**Untitled
1968**

Flowers with Vases
1966

Hillside Vineyard

**Ohio Farm
1988**

**Paradise at Dume
1982**

Memorabilia

Margaret's Art Table

Made in England
Bone China

Made in England
Candlestick Holder

Margaret's Prayer Book
& Wedding Announcement

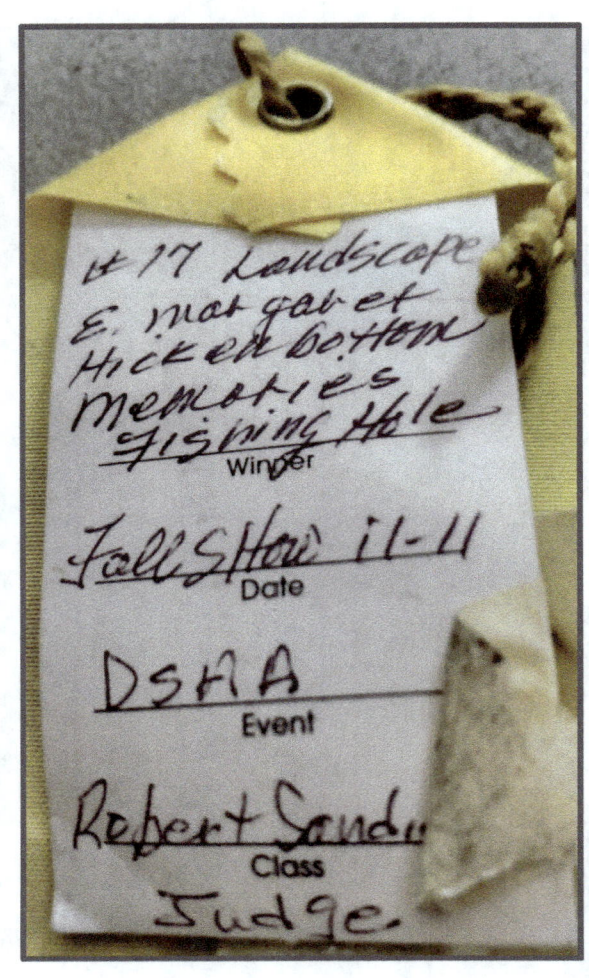

**DSAA Award
for Memories | Fishing Hole
November 11, 2011**

PART TWO

Wem, England

**Life isn't about finding yourself.
Life is about creating yourself.**

— George Bernard Shaw

Wem, Margaret's beloved Wem. She will say often, "Son, take me to the train station. I want to go to Wem . . . please, son."

Each time Keith will in a sincere and kind manner respond saying, "Mom, the trains aren't running, today."

Today, in the year 2022, Margaret is a resident in a permanent memory care facility three blocks from Keith's home.

The caregiver says Margaret speaks aloud during the night to Ethel — an older sister who died many years ago. Margaret is overheard to say she wants to go home to Wem.

Margaret's childhood home in which she was the tenth and last born was in the northern part of Wem, four miles from the Welsh border north of The Irish Sea. Margaret may recall fleeting moments of remembering her life in Wem, her home and the sweet peas that once adorned the hillsides.

Long gone for a host of years until recently revived as noted in one of Margaret's books from her collection about Wem, in John Whitehead's book, *Wem Now & Then*, it is stated . . . "the sweet peas came back into prominence by residents of Wem, Mr. and Mrs. Good of Weston, under Redcastle in 1988." *(Ref. 2)*.

Margaret is an avid reader of English history. *The Story of Wem and Its Neighborhood* by Iris Woodward, was no doubt read and re-read by Margaret, as its dog-eared pages reveal. *(Ref. 3)*. Its repairs are visible — the clear sticking tape now faded yellow, each page taped securely. Woodward's book, published at the request of the Wem Urban District Council, is a contribution to the Festival of Britain. Margaret has read this well-worn book, but she may not remember it as well today.

Prior to 1974 when the North Shropshire District Council local government reorganized the town, Wem ". . . was picturesque rural countryside considered as an urban district" as noted in the publication, *A Short History of The Parish Church, by Wem Parochial Church Council.* *(Ref. 4).* Margaret may, when reading, transport herself back in time. She is fond of history, and all of life in general, evidenced by her extensive book collection which includes topics ranging from religion, health, birding, fine art painting, self-help and improvements, guides to sewing, wood building know-how, and the history of England. Throughout her life, Margaret, with a proper English upbringing, brings to her table an American way of life, family values, her keen intellect, her wisdom, and while oftentimes adamant, she brings frivolity to her home with love and respect for her husband and family.

In many of Margaret's books are bookmarks placed throughout their pages. There are small cut pieces of paper, intricate designer store-bought markers, and leather strips engraved with gold-leaf — presumably gifts to her at birthdays and Christmas.

At 96 years of age, Margaret has not the physical ability to read her favorite books nor return to Wem. She may not as well be able to tell you all of Wem's history although she may relate that in earliest times, Wem was a borough with a charter grant.

Margaret's beloved Wem, District of Shropshire, England, is in size an area of 1 1/2 square miles, a total of 903 acres. In the 17th century, in the year 1677, a fire destroyed the town. Much later, in the 19th century, in the year 1846, roads improved the area and industry flourished. In the same year, a railway — the first in Wem — establishes convenience for the community.

Of a dozen or more interests of Margaret's, the Church of St. Peter & Paul Parish stands at the top of her proverbial 'To Do List' to visit again someday. It predates the 1677 fire and remains today. Of Wem's schools, the Adams Grammar School founded in 1650, served the community until the 1677 fire burnt it to the ground. It was rebuilt in 1776 and modernized in 1930. Its original name was The Old Grammar School. Margaret, born in 1926, would have attended Adams Grammar School. In 1950 the school celebrated its tercentenary.

Wem's town square is referred to as The Castle Field — a town center that once held a castle. Today, Wem's town hall hosts concerts, plays, and productions of local dramatic organizations. The main industry in Wem today is agriculture — creameries, breweries, corn mills, sawmills, joinery works, and chicken and egg farms. It has been noted back in the day that Margaret's father worked as a journeyman painter and decorator; her mother owned a store selling comics and periodicals, and was a newsagent, tobacconist, confectioner, and stationer.

The Parish Church of St. Peter & Paul, established towards the end of the reign of King Edward III, dates from the year 1582. Bells were important in the church as well as an English tradition, for in the parish's publication it states, "in 1680 a new ring of five bells cast. In 1768 a new peal of bells cast and rehung in December 1887." *(Ref. 4).*

In 1897 workers cast two more treble bells that are hung to commemorate Queen Victoria's Diamond Jubilee, making a total of eight bells today.

A renumbering of the bells occurred in May 1898. Between 1964-67 workers turned the bells, re-tuned the bells, and rehung the bells on a new steel frame replacing an old oak frame.

Margaret still loves her town, Wem — one can see why — its history and charm is apparent.

Margaret, known for her love of flower and vegetable gardening, may have used in her artworks the colors of the sweet peas that Wem was once known for. Revered by local townspeople, in 1988 the Eckford Sweet Pea Society of Wem began long after Margaret moved from Wem. Initially, at the turn of the century, Mr. Henry Eckford, a nurseryman, developed cross-breeding, new shades, and varieties of sweet pea that led to a saying in John Whitehead's book, *Wem Now & Then*. He quotes, "Wem, where the sweet peas grow." *(Ref. 2)*.

Margaret grew up in Wem's cottage neighborhood at 6 Aston Street where she and her family lived next door to her mother's parents. After the passing of her grandparents, the whole family moved there — to 8 Aston Street — a much larger home. Margaret's grammar school was located near a railway station. She was to learn that by the 1960s the railway stations were gone due to less usage by Wem's then-modern community; however, they are again in use today.

Wem's public land in the north side of town, once a marsh and moorlands noted for "crows and cranes," changed its usage for public citizens' recreation. The citizenry turned over their property deeds to the district for development of Wem. After slow improvements, modern day times see "tennis courts, bowling greens, toilets and pathways added." *(Ref. 3).*

Prior to Margaret's recent fall in September, 2022, which prompted her ambulance transport to the local hospital in Cameron Park, she was making ready to travel to Wem, saying to Keith, "Get me my pocketbook. I am going to Wem. Please, son, take me to Wem." Margaret places her brown hardbound suitcase on the floor in the hallway near Keith's front door. She is ready to go. She wants to return to Wem, her home in heart and mind and soul.

In addition to an increasing talent in painting major fine art in oils, Margaret has been an accomplished seamstress. She will sew with fabrics patterned of roses in colors of pink, yellow, and fuchsia for her wardrobe to wear around the house. Her collection of Simplicity and McCall patterns is stacked in drawers of her sewing room cabinet although her Singer sewing machine is idle now. Her collection of Betty Crocker cookbooks is now in packing boxes along with other full boxes double stacked. Her handwritten recipes, loose from their 6 x 9-inch wooden recipe box, lay still now out of her kitchen where she loved making special meals for friends and family when they all gathered to 'break bread'.

While at his mother's home recently when boxing up the pots and pans, the dishes, and the Tupperware from his mother's kitchen cabinets, Keith reminisced aloud about the good times they had there, saying, "There were times the family — all of us — Barry, Gerri, Chris, Kathryn, and Jeffrey, piled into Mom's kitchen around the stove in preparation for making ready our special holiday meals. Typically at Thanksgiving this was Gerri's homemade tamales, brought from her home and previously made with the help from her sisters. It was fun! We had good times."

Though her life may be near its end, Margaret colored her world with endearing memories of her life in love with Forrest, a mother's love for her family, and a longing for the scent of the sweet peas of Wem and the sight of the green, green grasses of home.

Epilogue

Today is a sad day.

Margaret passed on October 12, 2022, at 6:30 p.m., unexpectedly yet anticipated.

Today, October 13, 2022, is a day in remembrance of Forest's birthday, October 13-1921, at 6:45 p.m. He died on April 21, 2006.

He was 84. Margaret was 96.

We Were English War Brides

> *Newspaper Article:*
> *Los Angeles Herald*
> *May 8, 1985*
> *to commemorate the end*
> *of WWII on May 8, 1945*

September 22nd 1985, will mark our 40th wedding anniversary. I was an English War Bride, so my life changed dramatically. I was born in a small country town in Shropshire, England. My husband-to-be, from a rural area of Eastern Ohio. My home town of Wem, has it's roots reaching way back in history, having been mentioned in the Domesday Book, which was recorded in 1086. I have affection for my home town, even so I have never regretted leaving and coming to America.

Looking back, I now realise how young and immature I was, I jokingly say, "I was 19 going on 12." Of course at the time I thought I was fully grown. My first encounter into this new world was having to report to a camp in the south of England, Tidworth, on the Salisbury Plain. The group of war brides, which I was a part of, stayed at this camp for nine days. I have many happy memories of those days, especially the kindnesses we received from the American Red Cross nurses.

My first disappointment came when a new group arrived – and left before we did. Then, to add insult to injury, they would be travelling to America in style on the "Queen Mary". We were destined to go on the Willard H. Holbrook, referred to as a 'Kaiser cork'. I will never forget the awful experience of sea-sickness, which I managed to fall victim to within two hours of sailing time at Southampton, and continuing for seven of the nine days crossing time. April is not a good month to be crossing the Atlantic. As we were getting closer to New York City, we saw on the horizon the "Queen Mary" returning to England for more brides. This was the first time I had seen the famous ocean liner, but since moving to California was delighted when I was actually able to go on board.

We lived in Ohio for 16 years, I became a naturalized American citizen, thoroughly enjoying talking politics, and becoming part of the American way of life. We moved to California in 1962. This was a big undertaking — another journey into the unknown. Our 40 years together have been blessed with many happy times, with a deeper love and respect growing for each other along the way. We haven't escaped the heartaches, but we've always managed to rise above them, drawing closer to each other, with the determination to see it through. We have been blessed with three sons, and two grandsons, a third grandchild on the way, hopefully this time, a little girl.

Our future plans are looking forward to retirement, living in Northern California along with another visit to England, and to reminisce about the war years with family and friends in old familiar places.

E. Margaret Hickenbottom
Simi Valley, California
May 8, 1985

Resources/References

Ref. 1
The Family Tree of Alfred Downes and Thorley Families. Genealogy compiled by George Downes (son of Arthur Downes, the brother of Margaret Hickenbottom. England), circa 1980.

Ref 2.
WEM Now & Then, a photographic essay by John Whitehead, The Adams Press Publication, 1992. England.

Ref. 3
The Story of WEM and its Neighborhood, by Iris Woodward, 1952, Wilding and Son LTD, Castle Street, Shrewsbury, England.

Ref. 4
A Short History of the Parish Church, Published by Wem Parochial Church Council to commemorate the Silver Jubilee of Her Majesty Queen Elizabeth II, 1977. Printed by Wildings of Shrewsbury Limited, England, circa 1977.

Ref. 5
Los Angeles Herald Examiner, May 8, 1985. WWll ended on May 8, 1945. The Los Angeles Herald Examiner asked readers to submit their memories of when the War ended and Margaret Downes Hickenbottom's entry was published under "We Were English War Brides."

Dates of Importance

1582
Parish established, St. Peter and Paul Episcopal Church, England.

1680
Parish bells are cast.

1677
The great Wem Fire, England.

September 27, 1853
Birth of Emma (maiden name unknown) Downes, mother of Alfred Downes.

August 18, 1878
Birth of Alfred Downes.

1882
Birth of Eleanor Mary Thorley.

1887
New parish bells are cast.

1897
Queen Victoria's Diamond Jubilee.

1898
Renumbering of parish bells.

1902
Birth of Charles Downes, brother of Margaret.

1903
Birth of Harry Downes, brother of Margaret.

April 21, 1903
Death of Emma Downes, mother of Alfred Downes.

1905
Birth of Percy Downes, brother of Margaret.

1909
Birth of Mona Downes, sister of Margaret.

1913
Birth of Walter Downes, brother of Margaret.

1915
Birth of Ethel Downes Blake, sister of Margaret.

1917
Birth of Arthur Downes, brother of Margaret.

1919
Birth of Nellie Downes, sister of Margaret.

October 13, 1921
Birth of Forrest Hickenbottom.

1922
Birth of Edna Downes, sister of Margaret.

September 5, 1926
Margaret is born.

August 12, 1933
Death of Alfred Downes.

June 6, 1944
Invasion of Normandy, France, WWII.

May 6, 1945
VE Day and end of WWII.

September 22, 1945
Forrest and Margaret marry.

January 3, 1946
Forrest arrives back in America.

April 1946
Margaret relocates to America.

1955
Margaret and Keith travel to Wem.

1962
Forrest, Margaret, and family move to Simi Valley, California.

January 25, 1965
Margaret attends Adult Education Program Simi Valley, California.

August 26, 1965
Margaret is awarded a Certificate of Completion of 30 Business Hours, Beginning Drawing & Painting, Simi Valley, California.

January 27, 1966 – June 4, 1968
Margaret takes Advanced Drawing and Painting day and evening classes, Simi Valley, California.

1969
Death of Eleanor Mary Thorley Downes.

June 11, 1974
Margaret receives a Certificate of Appreciation in recognition of devoted valuable service rendered to Valley Vista Convalescence Hospital.

1977
Queen Elizabeth II's Silver Jubilee.

1987
Forrest and Margaret move to Clearlake, California.

1988
Sweet Pea Society Established, Wem, England.

1998
Forrest and Margaret move to Cameron Park, California.

April 21, 2006
Death of Forrest Hickenbottom.

November, 2011
Margaret wins 4th Place D.S.A.A. Art Award for Memories | Fishing Hole.

April 26, 2012
A memorial is held for Forrest at El Dorado Community Church, Placerville, California.

April 25, 2014
Death of Jeffrey Hickenbottom.

October 12, 2022
Death of Margaret.

February 9, 2023
Life Celebration is held for Margaret at El Dorado Community Church, Placerville California.

Acknowledgments

My heartfelt thanks and appreciation to Keith Hickenbottom, for his permission to author my story of my view of his mother, and for inviting me to meet her in his home during 2021 and 2022.

My appreciation to Barry Hickenbottom for sending me his collection of the Hickenbottom family historical records and history archived by his cousin George Downes of England for my use in drafting my story.

And for you, Gerri Hickenbottom, I remain delighted to add you in the grand scheme of things. You have made an impression in being a dutiful and loving daughter-in-law to Margaret.

In actuality, I believe both you and Barry have been the go-to designated family members in helping Margaret with many of her personal and healthcare needs — the chocolates sent to her in the mail, the daily newspaper subscription for her, the hair salon appointments, medical visits both you and Barry attended to, and the weekly phone calls placed to stay in touch with Margaret to say hello and to ask, "How Are You?" from your home eight hours away in Southern California.

Both Chris and Kathryn personally assisted Margaret in her later years at Cameron Park.

And for you, Keith, who opened your home for your mother as her safe haven when she could not stay alone, it is hoped my story brings to mind the happiest of memories and the happiest of times in spite of the hardships that caring for a loved one diagnosed with dementia and Alzheimer's disease brings one to bear.

— **Sandy Benson Castillo**
April 2024

Other Books of Interest by Sandy Benson Castillo

Southern Charms:
    A Collection of Stories by a 'Bama Gal
    2010

A Southerner's Companion:
    Poems From Out West
    2010

A Cast of Characters:
    Life Chronicles of Family and Friends
    2013

The Long Haul
    The Story of Roger Willeford
    2013

Sandy Benson Castillo

About the Author

Sandy Benson Castillo's previous books include self-published historical memoirs of family and friends, and a book of poetry.

Having worked for 38 years in the 9-5 workplace in the medical insurance field, Sandy is now retired.

Originally from South Alabama, she currently lives in Northern California, where she spends time gardening, visiting with family and friends, traveling, and creative writing.

To Contact the Author
please email:
Sandy Benson Castillo
vicsanc@comcast.net

For Direct Book Orders
please contact:
www.Lulu.com

To Contact the Publisher
please email:
Karen Mireau
Azalea.Art.Press@gmail.com

www.ingramcontent.com/pod-product-compliance
Lightning Source LLC
LaVergne TN
LVHW020947090426
835512LV00009B/1739